EASY-READ FACT BOOKS

Airports

Andrew Langley

Franklin Watts

London · New York · Sydney · Toronto

© 1987 Franklin Watts

Franklin Watts
12a Golden Square
London W1

First published in the USA by
Franklin Watts Inc.
387 Park Avenue South
New York, N.Y. 10016

Franklin Watts Australia
14 Mars Road
Lane Cove
NSW 2066

Phototypeset by Keyspool,
Limited
Printed in Hong Kong

UK ISBN: 0 86313 602 8

US ISBN 0–531–10445–1
Library of Congress Catalog
Card No: 87–61351

Design:
Janet King
David Jefferis

Illustrations:
James Dugdale
Christopher Forsey
Michael Roffe
Studio Briggs

We wish to thank the following
individuals and organizations for
their help and assistance and for
supplying materials in their
collections:
British Airports authority
British Airways
British Caledonian Airways
Jilian Burgess
Iberia Airlines
IBM (UK) LTD
Lockheed-California Co
Lufthansa
Oshkosh Truck Corp
MV Philips Co Ltd
TWA
Zefa

Note: The majority of
illustrations in this book
originally appeared in
"Airports" An Easy-Read Fact
Book.

11.95

Contents

The first airports

Early aircraft were small and light. They could take off and land on short grass runways. So the first airports were just large flat fields with control towers and hangars to house the aircraft.

Control tower

Windsock

4

Passenger lounges at London Airport in 1946

An airfield in the 1930's

A modern airport

Here is a modern airport. The control tower is in the center. People in the Control tower tell the aircraft when to land or take off. Near it are the terminal buildings for passengers to enter and leave the airport.

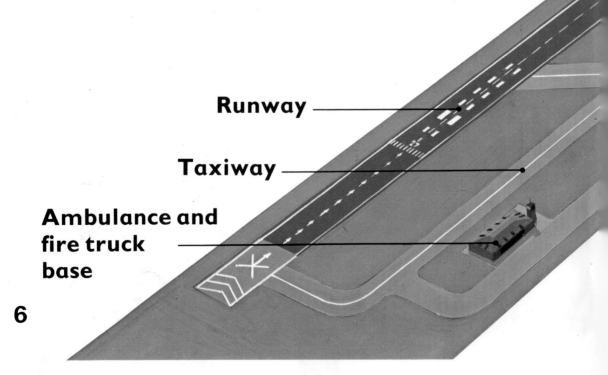

Runway

Taxiway

Ambulance and fire truck base

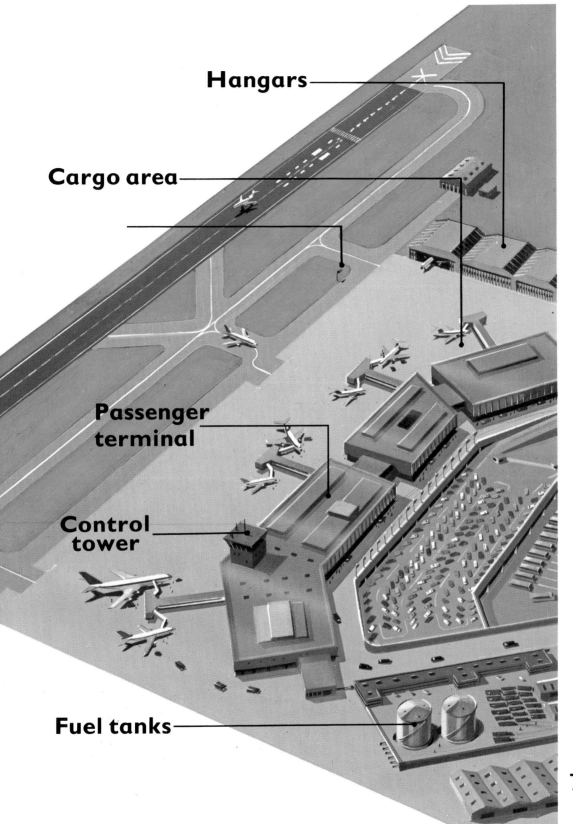

Hangars

Cargo area

Passenger terminal

Control tower

Fuel tanks

7

Buying a ticket

Before you can go on a plane you must buy a ticket from a travel agent or airline office. The ticket will show the time and number of your flight. You should plan to arrive at the airport about an hour before the plane is due to take off.

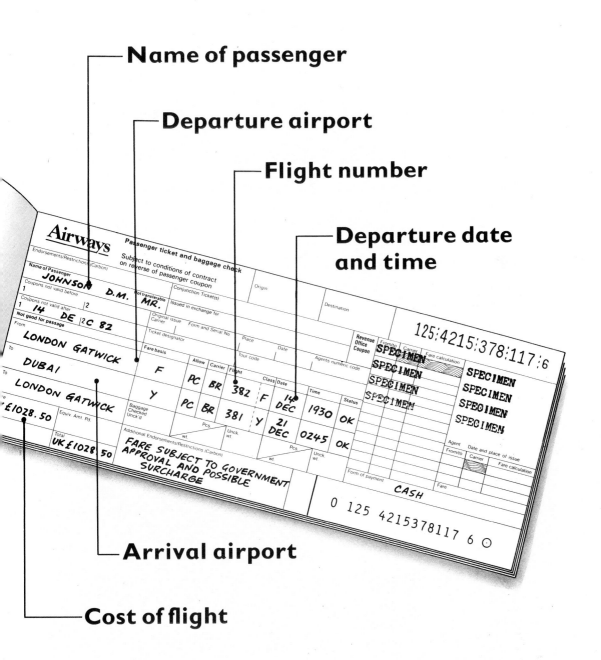

Name of passenger

Departure airport

Flight number

Departure date and time

Arrival airport

Cost of flight

9

Check-in

You should go first to the check-in desk and show your ticket. You will be given a boarding pass. Your baggage is given a label which shows the plane it should go on.

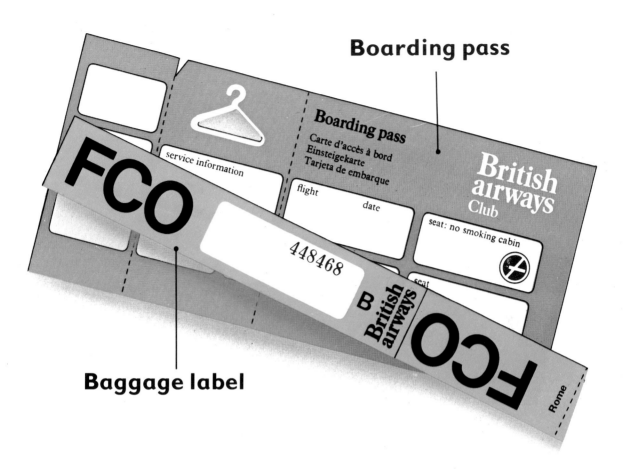

Boarding pass

service information

Boarding pass
Carte d'accès à bord
Einsteigekarte
Tarjeta de embarque

British airways Club

flight   date

seat: no smoking cabin

448468

seat

FCO

FCO

British airways B

Rome

Baggage label

VE 0036 IC
dian Airlines

Baggage being loaded on to a plane

11

Boarding a plane

You now go to the departure lounge. Everyone must walk through a metal detector to make sure that nobody has bombs or guns. Hand-baggage is put through an X-ray machine. You now walk along a jetty on to the plane.

Preparing for flight

The aircraft is refueled and its engines, tires and brakes are checked. The cabins are cleaned. Fresh food and drink is brought on to the plane.

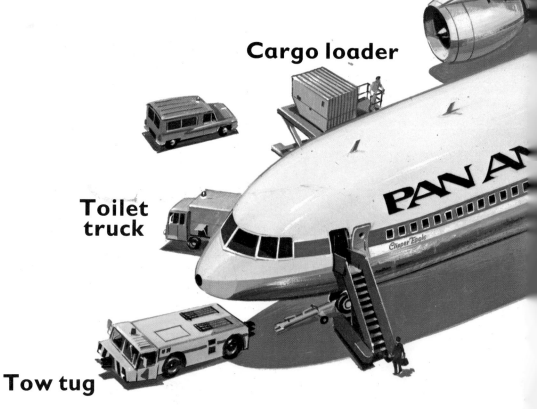

Fuel tanker

Cargo loader

Toilet truck

Tow tug

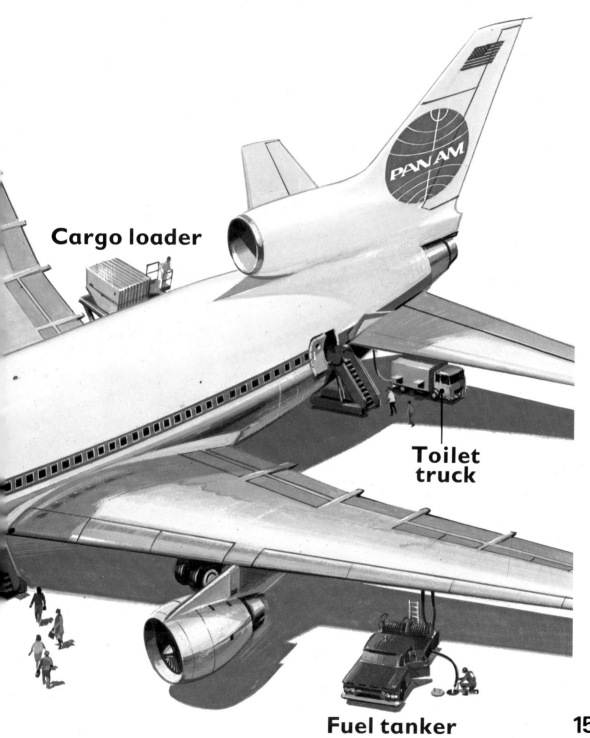

Cargo loader

Toilet truck

Fuel tanker

15

In the control tower

The people in the control tower are in charge of all movement on the ground and in the air. In the Airport Control staff direct planes on the taxi-ways and runways. In the Approach Control staff guide the planes in the air toward the airport.

Airport Control

Approach Control

Each operator in Approach Control keeps track of several planes at once. Operators only work for two hours at a time before needing a half-hour break.

Ready for take-off

Every pilot works out a flight plan showing the route to be taken. The route may be changed because of bad weather. It is checked in the control tower.

1. A tow tug pulls the plane from the parking bay.

2. The plane taxis down the taxiway.

The pilot must get
permission from the
control tower, to start
the engines and
move the plane.

3. Planes wait their
turn to go on the
runway.

4. The plane speeds
down the runway
and takes off.

Coming in to land

Before a plane reaches the airport the pilot asks Approach Control for permission to land. Only one plane can land at a time. The others circle around the airport as they wait their turn to land. At night the runway is lit up.

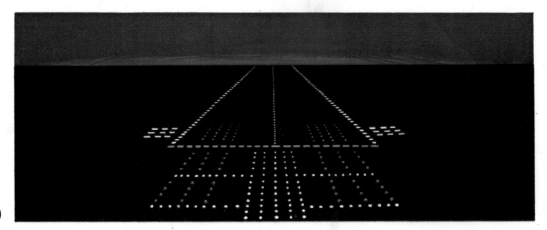

Once a plane has landed, it taxis off the runway. The engines are switched off. Then the passengers get out and their baggage is unloaded.

Ground services

Every airport has many special vehicles and services. They help to keep the airport running smoothly and safely.

Hydrant truck: To pump fuel into aircraft fuel tanks

Snowbrush: To clear light snow falls

Tow tug: For pulling a jumbo jet

Planes are inspected and are serviced in hangars at the airport. This must be done very quickly.

Emergency!

Flying is very safe, but accidents do happen. The most dangerous parts of a flight are taking off and landing. Fire and ambulance crews are always ready to go into action. The fire trucks carry foam to spray on a burning aircraft.

Firecrews must practise with their equipment.

Fire tender: Its "gun" can spray foam 300ft (92m)

25

Airline markings 1

There are more than **500** airlines in the world. Each one has its own colors and markings. These are painted on the body and tail of every aircraft. Here are some of the biggest airlines. Which countries are they from?

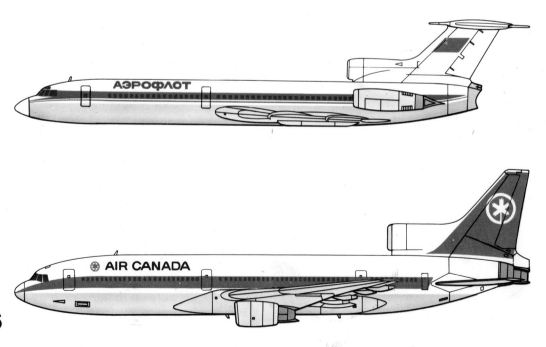

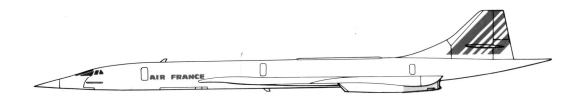

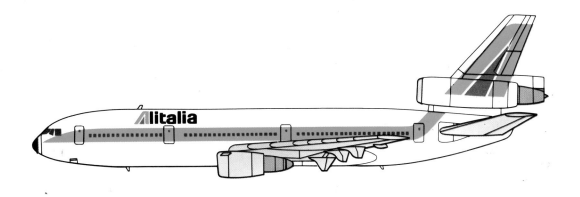

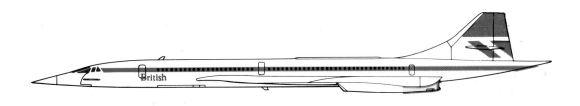

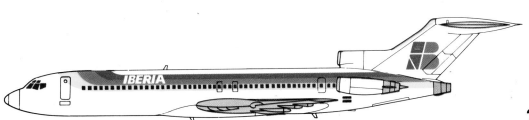

27

Airline markings 2

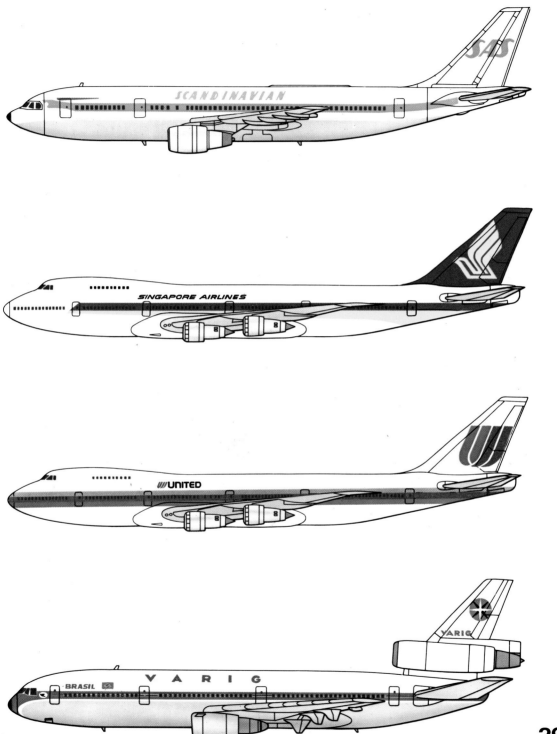

29

Airport facts

There are about 800 airports in the world for international flights. There are many smaller ones used by business and private planes.

The world's busiest airport is O'Hare in Chicago, Illinois. Every year it handles nearly 50 million passengers and 750,000 takeoffs and landings. That's one every 42 seconds, day and night!

Airliner tires are filled with nitrogen, a gas which will not catch fire. On landing, the brakes may become red-hot. If the tyres were filled with oxygen they would burst into flames.

The world's largest airport is the King Khalid International Airport in Saudi Arabia. It covers an area of 86 sq miles (221 sq km). Its control tower is 243 ft (74 m) high – also the world's largest.

The fastest airliner is the European Concorde. It can travel at speeds of up to 1450 mph (2333 kph).

The Boeing 747 Jumbo Jet is the largest passenger aircraft in service. It can carry up to 500 passengers. When flying the Atlantic it uses about 120 tons of fuel – enough to take a small car fifty times round the world.

Glossary

Some technical words are used in this book.
This is what they mean.

Boarding pass

A ticket given to passengers.
No-one is allowed to board a
plane without one.

Control tower

The building from which all
aircraft movements on the
ground and in the air are
controlled.

Jetty

A mobile tube through
which passengers walk to
board the aircraft.

Galley

The kitchen of an aircraft
(or ship).

Hangar

A big shed in which an
aircraft is stored and
repaired.

Radar

A way of detecting distant
objects by use of radio
waves. The objects show up
as yellow blips on the radar
screen.

Taxiway

Track along which the
aircraft "taxi" or move onto
the main runway.

Terminal

Airport buildings through
which passengers and air
freight arrive and leave.

X-ray machine

A machine which shows only
metal objects.

Index